Regret
R y a n S p o o n e r

**LETTERED
STREETS**
press

Chicago, IL | Seattle, WA

Regret
Copyright © 2014 by Ryan Spooner

Published by The Lettered Streets Press:
J. Young, A. Zimmer, I. Denning, M. Young

ISBN 10: 099118632X

ISBN 13: 9780991186327

No part of this book may be reproduced except in brief
quotations and in reviews without permission from the
publisher:

Regret
2014, Ryan Spooner

Cover design by Ryan Spooner
Interior design by the editors & by Tyler Crumrine

The Lettered Streets Press aims to publish work we love &
want to see in the world. We aim to work with writers willing
to work & be out in the world. We aim to work with writers
who view publishing as a community, not as a means to an end.
All profits from this press go back into the press. The editors
make no money from this press. We are a collective of sorts, not
a business. We publish poetry, fiction, essays, & hybrid work.
These terms are relative. We like blurring. We like projects.

Chicago, IL | Seattle, WA

Regret

for Nate

TABLE OF CONTENTS

PROLOGUE

HOW WE ACT

This was me: a full-on buzz blooming, embarrassing myself in that moody bar.

My friend and I picked the place, a cramped cocktail lounge, to try to elevate the evening above the few hours of slobbish day drinking we'd already put in. Earlier, we'd barreled through a margarita pitcher over tacos, then a six-pack of cheap stuff at a mutual friend's apartment. One has the urge, after all that, to make the night surpass the day's precedent, break the pattern, offer a new mood. I slicked my hair to the side in a sharp part, straightened my shirt, buttoned it all the way up. She threw some eyeliner on and swapped her sackish handbag for a slim clutch.

The bar itself was long and narrow like a shotgun shack, a dim little joint in one of those burgeoning, hot-spot neighborhoods local tabloids always seem to rave about. It skirted a part of town that had been historically working class, the sort of neighborhood young people tend toward, allured by the grit and semi-danger. Its insides were polished, post-industrial. The high-top tables were all dotted with votives in small glass jars, the walls were exposed brick, and filament bulbs hung low on long wires, giving the place an amniotic glow.

I tend to like divier digs—dark, grimy places. I'm not sure why. I guess as much as there's no accounting for taste, there's not much use in trying to explain it either. Recently I've come to appreciate a cold drink as a ritual best observed simply, unburdened by pretense or, really, any effort whatsoever.

I ordered a martini. The interesting thing about ordering a martini is how bodily its specifics are: do you want it bruised, bleeding, dirty? Again: semi-dangerous, a way to take the martini, with its opulence, its polished stemware elevating it off the dirty bar, slumming just a bit.

On that bodily note, the cocktail glass itself seems vaguely uterine: its wide bowl and thin stem like a rough anatomical sketch. I used to make martinis for my mother. All in all, she drank them infrequently, and maybe it was just a phase, but for a period of time she kept gin in the house, and would occasionally try on the luxury of having me mix her drinks while she lay on the couch. She liked Bombay, as dry as possible, with an olive and an onion, if we had it.

It hasn't taken me very long to learn that I love the idea of a martini more than the martini itself. This is not to say I don't enjoy one from time to time, just that my enjoyment always seems performed, spurred on more by my want to take part in the mystique of it than by the taste itself.

"Vodka or gin?" the bartender asked.

"Gin."

"Vermouth?"

"Dry." I felt annoyed, pressed by his questions.

"Olive or twist?"

"Olive."

"Up?"

"Up."

He ducked away and got to pulling the various odds and ends my drink required, and I remember shaking my head for a moment, my mouth open, my brow furrowed. For whatever reason the exchange, quick as it was, rubbed me the wrong way. Maybe I'm easily annoyed when I've had a few, or perhaps just more principled than I typically am, but I felt exhausted by him and his questions.

I said something to the effect of "Hell, does he even know how to make one?" to my friend, my words bent and slurred just a bit.

H. L. Mencken called the martini "the only American invention as perfect as the sonnet." Maybe that's at the root of what upset me: all those options seemed like deviations from the practiced form. I spent unknown ages ranting to my friend about it—in her general direction, actually, as she grew bored of me or embarrassed, and turned away to merely half-listen after just a minute or so. What exactly I said is lost now, smudged out by time or alcohol's simple distortion. I do remember that I noted especially my distaste for the vodka option, citing my uncle, who pours vodka straight up into a cocktail glass and calls it a martini, which irks me.

To authenticate my doggedness, I harped on how my mother has worked in bars and restaurants my whole life. My gripes are hers, essentially, though I wear them proudly as central aspects of my own character. I picked them up and internalized them as children tend to do, playing parrot with a parent's knowledge long before any real meaning settles in.

"Ryan," my friend said. "Look at yourself. Look at how you're acting."

I looked around the bar. At a few of the nearest tables, couples in color-coordinated plaid and second-hand tweed coats looked up from their gimlets and sidecars at me. I had made a bit of a scene, but luckily the music was cranked too high for anyone to hear much of anything, even themselves perhaps, much less my lurching qualms about ordering a drink. After a moment they went back to pantomiming interest in one another. They probably all thought it was a date gone horribly wrong, or that I made their own dates somehow more horrible. All those twenty-somethings, like ourselves, dolled up in approximation of their parents' style, ordering bygone drinks simply for the sake-of. The sake of what?

With nothing left to say, I snapped back: "How? How am I acting?"

And all this is prologue, really, a way of arriving at that question, which, silly as it seems, sticks with me: how was I acting? How am I ever?

I'm told often I have too big of a personality, which is to say, maybe, too big of a self. I should have stuck to bourbon, probably, that good old Southern standard. It keeps itself simple: pour it in a glass, sip it slow, and that's that. My friend was uncomfortable sitting next to me. I still hadn't taken my seat, and was pacing just a bit, actually. I was too "on": wearing an exaggeration of my own personality, broadcasting too much of my self, perhaps. My friend was "on," too, performing herself, though for her this meant an awkward avoidance of my energy, a nervous laugh and a prim, embarrassed scan of the room.

"My cup runneth over," the Psalms say.

With what? With self.

Not long after, she and I stopped hanging around one another very often. Not because of that night—not necessarily, at least. Our group of friends started to fracture a bit, as they tend to. She and her boyfriend broke up. I ended a long, complicated relationship with one of our mutual friends. Everyone went one way or another. Or nowhere. Young people have a flair for, a tendency toward the tumultuous. I may know that, but I don't think I'll ever learn.

Such a wonderful thing, *self*—here we are, so full of it.

I

RED PLATFORMS

The pair my mother owned: patent leather, a lustrous red the color of deep bruises, a short brassy zipper on the side. I would hold them, measure their heft, guess their dense weight like a carnival trick. My fingerprints smudged the slick red leather easily. They had dark wood heels, platform toes, and a round rough patch stuck like a decal to each sole for traction.

These were her favorites for a time. She'd wear them out on weekends, or on dates, or on nights out after working a dinner shift, stopping home to drop her apron by the door, change outfits in a flurry, and head out again.

Some evenings, while she waited tables, I would try them on—slide them over my white socks, mismatched and pilled from boyish carelessness, and tug the zipper up. The deep knock of them with each step on the hardwood was a gorgeous thing, lending terrible urgency—banging at the door, a heart beating—to even a few strides across the room or down the hall, where in a full-length mirror I'd watch myself turn them coyly on their toes. And the height—three inches or four—felt monumental, like a stilt walk.

In Rilke's novel *The Notebooks of Malte Laurids Brigge*, young Malte digs through bins and wardrobes filled with gowns, waistcoats, ornamented uniforms and theater costumes, trying them on—before a mirror of course—to sate the itch of wanting to be someone else for a while:

> Oh, how I trembled to be in the costume, and how thrilling it was when I actually wore it; when something emerged from the gloom, more slowly than oneself, for the mirror did not believe it, as it were, and, sleepy as it was, did not want promptly to repeat what it was told; though at length it had to, of course.

Did these shoes constitute a costume for me? I'm hesitant to say so, recoiling from the Batesian implications of donning my mother through her clothes. The shoes didn't transpose onto me some aspect of her, some essentialness. Quite the opposite actually. They seemed alien to my ideas of her, unlike any side of her I knew. They were a costume for her. At the time, they seemed to me impossibly adult—slick shoes to catch the eye of a stranger, call him over—but now I associate the memory of them entirely with her youth. She was not much older than I am now, if not the same age, and not yet given over to the deep regret she cultivates now of having grown into early middle-age.

And unlike Malte's dresses and frocks, these shoes weren't *forgotten*, not in the least. My fascination was instead with the newness of them—how one day she proudly plucked them from a boutique shelf, wore them out of the store, her previous pair floating loose among crinkled tissue paper in a deep, green bag. They were, I think, the sort of addition to a wardrobe that blinds you a little. They were new, and she loved them because of it, and her joy over them persisted for as long as they fit her style. My trying them on, though, the act of it: I'm unsure what else to say about that. I'm unsure what it means that I would play such a tender action so close to the vest, keeping it hidden, private, reserving the practice of it until, at least for the evening, she was gone.

THE ILL FIT

The first outfit I remember assembling myself and really loving was a hodge-podge of what were then my favorite clothes: a long-sleeved, white cotton T; a green golf shirt over that, fully unbuttoned, the collar beat up by a year or so of hard wear; a pair of loose blue jeans frayed at the cuff and split across one knee; and a pair of Velcro sports sandals winched tight around my feet. I was nine years old. I put it all on and primped before the mirror, standing on the tub's white ledge to get a full view.

Later it was a pea coat, an honest-to-God one, inherited from an ex-Navy friend of my mother. She bought it cheap from him at a collaborative rummage sale. It likely cost her the bulk of what meager profit she turned that day selling her old platforms or worn corduroys, even though he discounted the price of it from what he would've charged a stranger. It was thick wool, double-breasted, with wide buttons emblazoned with anchors. It came with the condition that I sometimes, especially when wearing the coat in his presence, offer an ear for his Navy stories to cover the remaining cost, which I did happily.

But clothes, for most of my childhood, stoked the ridicule of other kids at school, who, musing on a frayed shirt or pair of busted tennis shoes, could compose great works in that grimmest of genres—taunts. I got by with thrifted clothes mostly, or flawed, surplus pieces my mother could buy for cheap at garishly lit warehouse stores. Their insults seemed so effortless, so off the cuff (so to speak), that in my mind there must have been a good deal of cruelty just coiled up in the clothes I wore, waiting for a switch to be thumbed so it could spring out.

One example, perhaps not the best, but the most readily conjured: it was spring. A Southern spring, already hot and muggy in April, the days dampening more and more toward hurricane season and, with it, the daily top-out of humidity, the five-o-clock storms that set in each evening for an hour or so, booming eastward down toward the coast. I wore a thick sweater, brown or dark gray, and a pair of coarse, black jeans to school, and tried as best I could to pass the day without catching any criticism, because I felt, should that happen, that I would have broken to pieces.

How much of this was imagined, my own self-conscious worry acting as an echo chamber? Or, supposing they were so mean, to what degree is it now warped, doubled in size, in meanness, for the simple fact that it's stuck with me since then? In truth, I could be equating an honest "Why are you dressed that way?" with the more crushing "Don't you know it's spring, idiot, not winter?" Discomfort is an untrustworthy lens.

I felt ashamed and uneasy: that much I remember clearly, somewhat because the heat that day was unbearable, but more so because I always meant for my clothes to hide me, in a way, or at least to hide how poor my mother and I were. The slightest comment, the smallest second glance in the middle of a day, and I felt exposed. That morning, getting dressed, there had been a tradeoff in front of the mirror. This particular outfit, the denim and the off-season wool, was all that had been clean enough for me to wear. The forfeiture of physical comfort, the invitation for a lacerating lesson in style—these were lesser perils than the exposure of my lower class. I would have rather been seen as an idiot incapable of dressing himself for the weather than as a poor kid whose mother couldn't afford the laundry that week. I took it on the chin, mostly, with sustained, concerted effort. Though, no matter the mental steeling I might have managed, a child is a child, and children both give and receive cruelties with violent efficiency. But what broke my heart most was that, after the initial doubt, I had come to like how I looked in those clothes. I stood in the mirror primping, shifting the bulky sweater—a cast-off from my mother's artist friend, Zeke—fiddling with the rise of the jeans copped for a few bucks at the Salvation Army. *This is fine*, I might have thought. No: *This is good*.

Clothes were hard to come by, growing up poor and absent an older brother to hand old garments down, and I picked out the deficits in my wardrobe probably more sharply than cliques of well-off classmates. I was aware of my clothes, and I was aware of theirs. They wore new pressed khakis each fall, or factory-worn blue jeans weathered in purposeful ways in only the most glamorous spots. They wore crisp white T-shirts under golf shirts or pale, button-down oxfords, and carried monogrammed LL Bean backpacks to school.

I was jealous of this last item for at least a few months following my first encounter, fifth or sixth grade it would have been. Ramsay Schrum carried one, and he was a tall, good-looking guy who started talking casually, openly, about drugs and sex a little too early, and who was therefore coolly dangerous and easily idolized. Monograms represented a particular kind of affluence, notable especially among the moneyed, Protestant families of the South: the initials themselves were a kind of currency marker, though signifying instead of dollar bills the storied wealth of a good name tied to a good family, its antebellum roots torn violently into the present by a little stitched letter, B for Bolling, or T for Turner, or D for Dixon. However much I try, though, I can't remember Ramsay's middle initial, even though I'm sure I must have stared at it semi-daily, squeezing myself down the crowded halls of my middle school.

After a while, I stopped wanting one of those backpacks, replaced my desire with disgust. By the time, years later in college, I dated a Georgian girl of good birth, a debutante, my gentle disdain had turned to outright spite: I noticed her initials embroidered on little orange hand towels draped over the silver bar in her dormitory bathroom, and then on the large canvas tote she carried with her to the beach just a short drive from campus, and then, of course, on her LL Bean backpack. I commented on her monogram often, noting its silliness, revealing my bitterness toward the affluence I thought—still think—it suggested. I nagged her at every chance, I'm sure. My insistence was a kind of tell, and in the end, this small detail, and my inability to move beyond it, turned indicative of what would become our most irreconcilable conflict: the impassable rift of class, marked out cleanly, like the blue on maps, by purchases. Things wanted, things got.

In high school, I wore a uniform, a white golf shirt and pair of khakis, an even tuck around the waist, a brown belt, and white sneakers. Uniforms made the morning shuffle easy—fewer options, less anxiety over what to wear. This is what the proponents always say, at least, citing the cruelty and competitiveness of children as good reason to do mostly away with variation in dress, to ease an uneasy existence, level the playing field, so to speak.

Though for me the anxiety lived at night. Each night, I'd wash the white shirt in the tub, a drop of bleach in the hot water, hang it to dry on a wire hanger by the box fan. The growing, deepening sweat stains in the armpits, the ring of grime on my collar's top ridge, though, broadcasted more and more just how often— every day—I wore that shirt, and, no matter the scrubbing, just wouldn't bleach out.

My mother has always prided herself on the fineness of her taste in clothes. She told me a story once about the fur coat her mother bought her when she was a girl. Told me several times. This story is an old standard for her, a kind of mantra to hold off the creeping disdain she feels for my grandmother, now dead, and whose character is therefore limited only to what one can remember.

She found a fur coat in a mail-order catalog and came, in the following months, to fixate on her desire for it. She pleaded relentlessly for it: all through the weeks surrounding her early October birthday, past Thanksgiving, and all toward Christmas, she pestered my grandmother. But the answer was always no. I'm not sure what it cost, but whatever it did was too much for the family to afford. The painful thing about wanting a gift so badly, especially as a child, is the mix of hope and embarrassment that overwhelms you until the moment comes to tear off the wrapper. Every "no" becomes, to a hopeful child, a possible part of the ruse. A parent's sternness becomes a part of the play, no sure answers coming until you pry open the box.

On Christmas morning, my mother and her five brothers and sisters piled into the den to open their presents in front of the woodstove where, baking dry from their snowball fight the day before, lay the white sports socks they'd used as mittens. The night before, they'd been allotted their single gift, a favorite running joke of my grandparents': a new pair of pajamas, which they were required to wear to bed in preparation for the photographs to be taken the next morning, and which they wore now, tearing through all that wrapping paper.

My mother got her fur coat of course. Hidden in a small unassuming box near the back of the tree. What did that moment look like? For the life of me I can't picture my mother overcome by excitement or joy, losing herself in a moment, especially not in the colossal way that children do. I know her as wry and cool, a little stoic, a vice grip tightening down on any outward expression. I think, early on, she was chastised by her parents against, or maybe accused by a lover of being, "that" kind of girl: hysterical, or giddy, or simply emotional. In short, warned against being a person alive in this world.

My grandmother spent the better part of an hour the night before squeezing the coat into that cramped box. I imagine her, knees down on the shag as though to genuflect, kneading and folding the fur to make it fit. A trying process, but a sensual one too. I'm remembering the dreaded ordeal of tucking and stuffing, pressing and rolling, pinching and praying that was required to coax my sleeping bag back into its nylon compression sack whenever we broke camp out west, and how, though the work made me manic with impatience, the payoff of using my hands was well worth the trouble. More likely, though, my grandmother undertook the task idly, sitting on the plush floral sofa and watching television, using her hands slowly, deliberately, the way she used to pick though beans and black-eyed peas for little stones all afternoon. This trims away much of the magic of the gift, I think, envisioning her likely lack of urgency: it dilutes the sweetness by some small amount. But people, real people—not the enlarged, distorted memories that outlast them—have a way of doing that, don't they?

My mother hated my grandmother for many years. As a teenager, my mother was headstrong, volatile, and pregnant, and my grandmother was spiteful and dramatic. They had blowout fights, both physical and verbal, that resulted in my grandmother wailing for her husband to save her and my mother storming out to run away for a while. But I could tell that when she told this story, my mother realized it hadn't always been that way. This story was a way for her to keep that fact safe from all the trauma packed firm into her troubled sense of "mother." And when her mind began to pull toward this story—"This reminds me of that time . . ." "Have I ever told you . . . ?"—as it did each year around Christmas, it was another year her mother had been gone. When I was young, I could tell she regretted nearly everything about her relationship with her mother, but that year by year she became more and more resigned to the fact that there really was nothing to be done.

The coat: I saw it once, I think, tucked into a trunk or crate in the attic of one of my many childhood homes. We want a thing so badly, then we have it, have our euphoria too, and for a period of time it's prized among our most beloved possessions, it having been one of our seemingly greatest needs. Then it's packed away, and we move on to the next.

The want for finer things is often worn down to nonexistence in boys, who are supposed to not care about appearance, at least not in that way. In me, though, the desire to have and wear what I want was picked out early, then laid away, like the school clothes my mother would begin making payments toward as early as June. It late-bloomed, and today I spend probably too much on clothes. I resist AB's goading toward thrift shops and discount stores when she wants us to get out of our apartment for an afternoon or so. She takes my reluctance as an overly cold rejection, and we get in little spats about it here and there. I prefer instead to spend, really spend, to pay in full and, once the rush of the purchase has worn away, to try not to worry too much about the overpriced contents of my shopping bag. In stores, I'm flippant at the shirt rack, or the deep stacks of denim, or the piled boxes of shoes.

Max Beerbohm called the dandy "the child of his age," meaning perhaps, by "child," the product of his time and his surroundings, his fancies dictated by his context. Perhaps he properly meant the *child* child: a man infantilized by the power of his desire, his nagging want for something pretty, something new.

BROWN BOOTS

I was cleaning my brown boots this morning, working a slick ointment of mink oil and pitch into each bend and nook, running it over all the tight stitch lines and the low tuck of leather around the wood heel's edge.

These are a serious pair of boots. They are workish—a thick heel, a wide toe—a quality which, mixed with their overall gussied look, gives them a rugged prissiness. This is probably what drew me to them in the first place. I slipped impulsively into the store, a small shop on some Chicago corner—just for a look, I told myself, though in truth I fully expected (hoped) to be lured into some hasty buy. It was early fall, and in addition to feeling the first heaves of that slow spiritual nosedive toward winter, I was feeling a chill around my ankles. I needed something to make myself feel better. I needed some boots.

Plus, they were a good brown. Still are. They sat on their little notched display platform, all leather upper, all leather sole, all leather everything, hinting at warm wood-tones: polished hardwood floors, or oak-aged spirits—a bold whiskey in a short glass. Or a brown mug, maybe, of brown coffee, a dot of cream slowly browning in the middle, all that. Brown, brown. And I bought them.

That was some time ago now. This morning, when I was cleaning them, daydreaming all through that rote task, I had a strange feeling—like I was stepping out on a spouse, like I was cheating. I felt the guilt growing slowly in my forehead, which was furrowed and turning hot. I assumed at first it was just my concentration collecting there, that I was focusing hard and that was that. But then I paused, gave myself a little breather, and realized what it was: there in the closet behind me were my hiking boots, the chunky old Asolos I've had for fourteen years now. And, honestly, I felt a little watched by them, as though in caring so delicately for this newer, nicer pair, I was betraying all that time I'd kept the old ones. I had built and propped up a sturdy sense of loyalty to them over the years, the sort that comes around "just because" once you've stuck with anything long enough. And there I was this morning, wiping it all away.

In my teenage years I was an occasional hiker, and took trips each summer for two weeks or so at a time with Jim Duffey, who was dating my mother's friend. Jim led groups of students from the middle school where he taught English and History into the backcountry of Colorado, say, or Utah, or Arizona. Before I ever met him, I met the idea of him. My mother's friend Kelly taught me to love him before I ever met him. We sat in her sunny living room—I was spending the day with her, I think, while my mother worked—and she just talked and talked, and I listened. They had dated years before in Pennsylvania, in their early twenties, and had at some point, for whatever reason, split. Right then and there she decided to get him back—"I should call Jim Duffey," she said. And she did. Then, within the month, he was down to visit.

We went many places over that vital half-decade or so, setting camp seven miles up a trail and milling around all that roughness for weeks at a time. Some habits come into a life at just the right moment—a particular context, a necessary state of mind—and impress themselves more firmly into one's character than they could have at any other time. Though I haven't had a proper hike—packing in, packing out, huffing and sweating under the weight of gear, guessing for good footholds and the path in the trail's wear to follow—I still think of this as an essential cog in my character.

Those hiking trips drove into me a love of walking—walking *just because*—which is a love I've maintained since, even though I don't hike so much anymore. I still enjoy a good even-paced lap, a wide circumference around my neighborhood, despite how different it is from beating my feet dogged up and down switchbacks in the Rockies. And that age was prime time for this sort of thing for another reason: Jim was the first male role model I had who, unlike the boys and young men in my family, was more than just a few years my senior, and who, unlike the men my mother dated, wasn't an easy target for any of my Freudian misgivings. He was just sort of there, suddenly, dating my mother's friend, innocuous but vital.

For over a decade, those boots carried the combined dust of each place I went, packed into every crack and tread, staining slightly orange the treated suede. Jim's ritual was to pack out handfuls of dirt or sand or loam from anywhere we set camp—scoop it into recycled jelly jars or old pomade tins which, back home, got slapped with a masking tape label and set solemnly on top of his bookshelf. I never had anything so decided, but I did participate, in my own way, in the pride of having touched all that same dirt. It seems silly now, but I loved the fact that, wearing those boots, I was also wearing a little bit of each place they'd been.

These days, the treaded, contoured right heel has pulled away from the shoe—all the way down to the arch—and the impact-muffling padding inside has been crumbling out all over the place. And that's the condition they were in this morning: half-destroyed, useless, and sad as ever, peeking out from the closet as I labored lovingly over my newer pair. I felt a sting of loyalty. But I wasn't sure what, really, I could do. I set down the brown boot I was working on, the oil-slicked cleaning rag. What can you do? I spun around in my office chair and closed the closet door. You turn your lover's photo down.

As a boy, shoes got phased out almost seasonally, worn to death or outgrown as quickly as I could lace them up, it seemed. Every few months, my mother and I would be off to the store, where I'd sit on a padded bench and try on off-brands, watch the scale on the shoe-sizer slide gradually up, watch my mother attempt to hide her worry over the cost. And I felt the worry too, because it was my body—growing larger, becoming rapidly unfamiliar to me—that was causing it all. And there just isn't much one can do about that.

There were trainer-style sneakers early on. Their aggressive, sporty aesthetic won me over hard, similar to the rough-treaded mountain bike with thick coiled shocks I coveted in the sporting goods aisle. Then there were rubber-bottomed canvas Converse, which of course I thought I had discovered all on my own, and in whose purchase I felt wholly unique. I wore—and grew out of—running shoes, tennis shoes, high-tops, low-tops, mid-rise casuals, plimsolls, Velcro-bound walking sandals, and knock-off Birkenstocks. Gobs of them, though worn and worked through one at a time, gradually, like a slow drip.

Shoes last a little longer now, and gather in piles at the bottom of my office closet. I still tear holes in the bottoms of my cheap imitation leather oxfords, or even the flimsy canvas casuals I prefer when the weather's warm—sometimes a pinky toe poking through the side, rubber stripping off from around the sole in busted flaps. They can't put up with how often or long or hard I walk.

Those old boots, the Asolos, were new once, too. And in fact, they too replaced a different, even older pair. Truth be told, I hated them at first. They had good ankle support, sure, better than I'd ever had, but the soles were hard and the waterproofed padding was more rigid than I was accustomed to. In the store the boots hadn't *seemed* so bad—I'd stood on a sloped plank of wood, done a lap or two around the aisle—and in reality they likely weren't. Kids are bitter about change, fickle about their feet. I whined a lot during the time it took to break them in, clomping down each trail with a tragic bearing.

I was thirteen, and a trip west was coming up—only a week or so until I'd board a plane to Colorado to kick around Arapahoe or Mohawk Lake, familiar haunts—and I hadn't realized until it was nearly too late that in the year since I'd last been hiking, my feet had grown out of my old boots. Jim took me out into the yard to find a nice small hill on which to test their fit and how they dealt with the requisite range of motion: no good, my toes kept sliding and bunching up in a cramped tangle, asking for trouble. We climbed in his truck and drove to the store, where he bought the Asolos for me, right then and there, with his typical brand of effortless kindness.

"You've got to have boots," he likely said, his generosity—his charity, really—packaged matter-of-factly. He never even gave me the chance to worry about them—they were mine, and that was that. I realize now I'm not sure I ever thanked him.

BOYS WILL BE…

Boys. I've never liked this phrase, the ease of its application, or how quickly it's dispatched to dismiss transgression: here cat-calling the quiet girl at recess, here snapping the strap of a classmate's training bra, here roughing up another boy for his lesser masculinity. What will boys be? Forgiven, in truth. Absolved with a nod, a knowing smile, a folkish tautology.

As a boy, I was obsessed with boyishness. I was fascinated by Rockwell's images of boys, and would spend hours lying on the den floor poring through a wide, hardbound book of his paintings: portraits, illustrations, magazine covers—a retrospective on his body of work, its place in American myth.

I reveled in those boys, their exaggerated rawness like a rallying cry, telling me what I was, what I wanted to be. We see them depicted often with mussed hair and blushed faces with scrambles of freckles and lost teeth. They leapfrog, black-eyed, over other boys, dirt and torn spots on their clothes. Or they run toward us, fleeing a marm or truant officer, a stolen pie in their hands, or clothes gathered around their naked bodies, still sopping wet from a skinny dip. So many of Rockwell's paintings, particularly the commission pieces done for magazine covers, are hemmed in by blankness: the central scenes fading to white borders meant to house article tag lines and the like. Though, seeing them back then without knowledge of that context (and even now, to some degree, despite it) I saw nothing but frontier, indefinite space for filling in with whatever impish narrative I could imagine.

Everything wrong to do seems possible in Rockwell. And in boyhood, too. My younger brother and I were, as a pair, big on roughhousing, but I was bigger. I often forced him to practice the absurdly dangerous wrestling moves we watched professionals do, showboating, on the television. I'd heft his then frail frame above my shoulders and toss him onto the couch, a bed, or a pile of pillows, always entertaining split desire: not to cause any real harm, but also to hurt him just as much as I could get away with. Barthes called wrestling a "spectacle of excess," and it was for us.

A few photographs exist—a kind of sequence—of my brother and me, both bare above the waist, with licked-on temporary tattoos haphazard on our skin. We arm-wrestle on the floor, gnash our teeth and bow our chests toward the camera. And in our posturing, even then, as small as we were, I see a sort of yearning toward savageness—the dream life of two little wild boys.

Boyish images abound and dot the landscape of my memory like Ozymandian monuments, imprints of pride that seem now laughably outdated. When I was very small, we visited often as a family the muddy banks of a wide, shallow river called Cane Creek. To this day, I remember myself quick and vivid in the muck, ducking to scoop dense clay with the blade edge of a hand, though, in photographs taken during that time, I am stumped, small, and bulldog-cheeked, waddling in the lapping water barely of my own accord, barely standing evenly, crying a little in distress. Not at all the rock of stoicism I seem to remember.

In another memory, I see myself in a light I'm more familiar with, and in a manner I've maintained throughout much of my life: discomfort in my prescribed boyish bearings. On a quick hop from Pittsburgh to Charlotte, the last leg of a flight back from a two-week trip to Colorado with seven or eight other teenage boys, one of my travel-mates, Bo—a wiry, martenesque boy, handsome with his brassy tan and light curls—noticed a blond girl our approximate age. Womanish in her calm, confident demeanor, she was boggling to behold after fourteen days of speaking amongst ourselves almost entirely in a common tongue of coded boyishness. Bo gave us a wink and, forcing dusky timbres through a cracked voice, and bowing his chest out no small amount, he leaned forward and across the aisle to introduce himself to the girl. Listening in, we learned she was visiting our city, our state, only for a brief time, a weekend or so, for a funeral in fact. Still, he stayed the course, and made conversation in all those flirtatious ways cocky young men do—nagging slightly, teasing a bit forwardly, injecting a bit of tension, interpersonal conflict—something to prove—even into the smallest small talk. I never understood what he intended to happen, there on the plane. Even though I know fully what he *wanted*, wasn't there a better time and place for all this?

Though, I suppose such things don't really bear understanding, just doing, sating whatever that ghost feeling is that makes boys want to do things just because we know we can, or that we're allowed to. He wore a sort of numb smile the rest of the ride, and as we disembarked and made our way to baggage claim, I asked him why he even bothered. "At least I talked to her," he said, like counting coup.

THE TAUNT

A schoolboy's enthrallment: to poke the body, its cold rigor, with the tip of a stick: to test for signs of life. We see a bird dead on the path between the house and the driveway, or a small, gray mole dropped on the patio as a gift from our tomcat. We take a twig in our hand and rock the body from side to side. We test our willingness to disturb, test our fascination with the dead thing, test death itself. We agitate, prod, attempt to shake it from sleep. We lull, touch lightly, call up memories of the first tenderness we come to know: our mothers lulling us to sleep. Here is a stick, here is my hand, here I am a catalyst. For what? For whatever might happen. Perhaps nothing at all. This is the taunt.

I cut my teeth on the dozens. In the cafeteria, the hallway, the mulch-padded playground—everywhere, my lips like whetted blades. Grade-school Spooner was fascinated by cruelty—how you can or can't get away with it—as many young boys are. We taunted and prodded one another's idiosyncrasies, shamed one another's bodies. This boy stammers, or cried once in gym class, or has an effeminate flair. This boy swims with his shirt on for fear of exposing his flabby, sagging chest—fatty boys are often feminized by their peers, always the word "titty" on the tips of locker room tongues, locker rooms where "woman" gets bandied like a slur.

I was this boy. I considered the bravado, the gestalt of shit-talk part of the male bonding experience, grander than the momentary sting of any one phrase. Though, maybe that grandeur was a delusion on my part.

The dozens. If you don't know it, it goes like this: in a semicircle, or a full-on ring, or in a kind of mob, boys crowd in, some watching, some performing. Two or three or however many boys—always boys, learning to be what we thought men were by learning to hurt how men should: quickly, fiercely, and with great poise, a kind of duelist's honor keeping it somehow civil. Girls did it too, I'm sure, though our circles were always hyper-masculine and overtoned by what seemed like a din of chest-thumping. Did we shy away from the girls? It strikes me now that, for all our public posturing, we likely hid ourselves away from them, somehow thinking that we needed to test ourselves against one another before so much as daring to speak to this girl or that girl in class. Back and forth, we traded insults, watched sidelong for our audience's reactions—how deeply did they laugh? how long?—watched our opponent's demeanor. What got to him? How to taunt again?

Everything was on-limits until it suddenly, obviously wasn't. A shed tear, a thrown punch, the crowd, as bloodthirsty as it often seemed, even shrinking away from the *too-far*. Stepping up meant laying yourself open to whatever the next guy could muster himself to say. Individual taste and conscience seemed the only restrictors, and, as I remember it, I was particularly tasteless. I liked cruel humor, all its haymaker gumption, all the edge of mouthing off, giving one's all to the art of the taunt. This is likely a pill of reassurance, quelling the cruelty somehow, but I think what drew me (still draws me) to ribs and comedic insults, roasts and outright off-color slams was the *audacity* of it all. To smash decorum, really smash it, and somehow glue it back, good as new, with the mellowing pretense of a joke. *It's just a joke*—that mantra everywhere, warding off heartache as best it can.

Your mother jokes were the most economical means to hurt, and their familiar, rote formalism helped dilute the poison just a bit, or at least cover its taste. It was not so much the level of pain inflicted that allured me—I didn't keep some graded scale to measure the slight, varied textures of a particular wince or furrowed brow. It was the ability to hurt, the tendency toward it and how the whole event, the performance, provided a means to forgive it.

Letting the taunts get to you, letting go the illusion of placid stoicism, meant losing the game. We pantomimed boredom with one another's insults, picked lint from our shirts, cleaned our nails and checked our watches, acting as though the shots skipped clean off. But it had to have been a con. Could we have been so numb? I'm not sure. Occasionally it ended in fights, nothing more than little scraps quickly and discreetly cleaned up. Sometimes it never properly began, and instead took place throughout the day, an offhand jab one morning inciting an extended bout, twelve rounds spanning first and second periods, lunch and recess, and into the afternoon until one boy or the other hopped on a bus and headed home, leaving the other to kick rocks around the courtyard until his mother's burgundy car slid up to the curb. Of course such a masculine discourse ends in dull solitude, a lonely boy waiting for his mother to scoop him up and take him home.

I practiced everywhere, memorized the best one-liners leveled against me, recycled them for new enemies—and, importantly, new audiences—altered them to fit my rhythms and sensibilities. Parsing the humor of a really good one was perhaps my first foray into studying style. What makes it work? How sharp the barb, of course, but also how tight the wit, the sentence sort of spring-loaded and set to blow on the slightest turn of phrase. I still remember more than a few, kept as they are in some deep pocket of memory carved into the self at that age, alongside multiplication tables and state capitals and other factoids and details cemented by rote memorization and daily contact. A few old favorites: your mother's armpits are so hairy, it looks like she's got Buckwheat in a headlock. She's so tall, she did a backflip and kicked Jesus in the mouth. She's so fat, she fell in love and *broke it*. Your mother's so short, she needs a ladder to tie her shoes.

Sometimes I'd step up and into my mother's car after a day at school and be met with that serendipitous tinge you find when bumping into a friend on the street just after wondering what they might be up to, or when the radio plays a song after you've spent an hour humming its chorus. She was the topic of nearly all my conversations with the other boys, abstracted and nebulous throughout the day, and suddenly here she was in the car, her server's apron and order book in the passenger seat.

Fourth grade, waiting in the lunch line for our mashed potatoes and peas, I turned and tossed one at another boy, Brandis: "Your mother's so skinny her nipples touch." I think I had to call his name once or twice—"Brandis! Hey! Hey, Brandis!"—in the same innocently nagging tone with which I would hang on my mother's shirt sleeve for attention.

I had not known Brandis very well. He was in my class, or a friend's class, or a class down the hall. I saw him often in the school's corridors and courtyards, a friend-of-a-friend, though we had never really spoken. I assumed he was game, so I instigated. *Your mother's so skinny her nipples touch.* He recoiled, his face a mix of annoyance and exasperation, disgust at the fact that I'd worked so hard for his attention just to cut him while he stood idly counting his quarters for milk. He postured, puffed his chest, and promptly lost the game: "Quit talking about my momma!" he yelled, a bit purposefully loud, drawing some quick, shocked looks from our peers and, unfortunately, the teachers proctoring the lunch line. One of the younger teachers pulled me aside. Around the corner, he scolded me, saying, "I don't know what it is, Ryan, but you've got this fascination with people's *mothers*," like a caricature of Freud. I wonder if I bowed up against his claim, took it as a sort of ineffectual rib. He'd have to cut deeper than that to get any faltering from me. Had he called it a fascination with mothers in general, he might have been nearer the mark. Had he found my own mother at the core, called out my fascination with her, I might have conceded the point.

The allure of the dozens was that I could turn my mixed feelings about my own mother against someone else. I was embarrassed by her age and profession among my middle-class friends at school. When we know how deep and how fragile our own love is, we can more surely find and exploit the loves of others. As boys, it drove us to attack the first and probably greatest loves of our lives: our mothers. Isn't it funny how, when not using feminine resemblances as material against one another—the lilting voice, the light step, any touch of the color pink—we spent our time defending and attacking the women we did happen to cherish?

Another time, in my fourth grade classroom —working on art projects, I think, sitting around low, hexagonal tables, drawing on wide sheets of grainy newsprint—I said something derisive, I don't remember what, to a classmate named Noah, a stocky, mumbling boy too big for his age. Perhaps it was something that rattled against those qualities. His head was so big, he didn't have dreams, he had movies. He was so fat, he got baptized at SeaWorld—look at me, even now I can't leave it alone. Anyway: "Your mother," he said in response. *Easy*, I thought, and turned it around: "Your *grand*mother."

The next moment lives in my memory strangely: somehow extended, drawn out, crawling, yet also sped up. It retains a kind of distorted, rushing stillness, the way moments of intense fear or adrenaline do. A zolly effect on memory's lens. He slides back in his chair. It croaks that horrible dirge of aluminum legs scraping into tile. He stands and rounds the corner of the table, though I can't tell if he moves quickly or if he calmly plods over. He's just there, his face close to mine. He grabs me by my neck, pushes my chair back on its two rear legs the way schoolchildren do to keep themselves entertained. He's crying. "Don't you *ever* talk about my grandma," he says through snot and tears. He doesn't hit me or hurt me. The teacher calls *Noah! Noah!* a few frantic times until he lets go. When all four legs hit the floor, I say something defensively spiked, like, "That was fun," and straighten my shirt.

The love of that kind of cruel performance persisted through adolescence, though it had altered its manner of expression. The circles of onlookers were gone, and so was the slapstick, the innocent love of a *good one*. Without that outlet of the schoolyard, without the mid-spring afternoons by the wide concrete steps that rose to meet the old brick school's portico, my habits matured into an old-fashioned argumentative bent that more and more I'm realizing is one of my defining flaws.

I argue with AB sometimes. Only once or twice have I dug deep and sincerely tried to hurt her, like some invisible crowd was urging me on. More and more these days our arguments have a meta tinge, and come front-loaded with self-aware rejoinders: *Here we go. Not this again. You always do this.*

I have argued with everybody I have been close with— friends, lovers, partners. No surprises here. Occasionally, mid-argument, I'll realize the vehemence with which I am trying to make my words really count, really cut.

I argue with my mother, always have—anywhere from a harmlessly competitive spat propped up by flashy, hollow rhetorical ducks and dives to a fight, a real fight, in which we care more about hurting one another than any semblance of proving a point. She and I are both contrarians, both love wordplay, and both refuse to give an inch on anything, no matter how small.

Once, after we'd come to a disagreement about something—the laundry, where to eat, I don't remember—she stormed off, slamming her bedroom door in an odd role reversal: I was sixteen, she was thirty-two. And as she did, I called after her: "No wonder none of your boyfriends want to stay with you."

I shocked even myself with how easily, how willingly, the words slipped out. These days, in lieu of getting downright hateful, I avoid speaking to her for months at a time. Instead, I let my anger fall away, eased by the convenient balm of setting the telephone aside for a while.

Mostly, I argue with myself. I am of two minds regarding most things, each half questioning the other, taunting to see how far the other side might go. Lately I have taken up a sort of measured self-goading. I don't quite "loaf and invite my soul," following Whitman's example. Instead I antagonize myself, tell myself I'm wrong, issue challenges to myself about anything at all. I should've spoken up more at a work meeting, or I should've been less of a bore out last night with friends, or, god, why didn't I make better small talk with that girl on the street? On some level, I must do it for fear that without the pressure of judgment (even my own) to drive me, I'll fall short of my own expectations.

I lost once. Cross-legged on a grassy patch in the playground, a boy, John, tapped a nerve a little too suddenly—we had just been sitting there, a few of us, not the slightest insult or taunt. I got physical. A great euphemism, that: *got physical*. I got *violent*. I threw the full weight of my body onto him, pinning him to the ground, his lanky form stabbing knees and elbows into my abdomen. To say I *got physical* is to play into the myth of sticks and stones. Afterward, adults would say that there had been no harm in the words, only in my fists. I knew that wasn't the case.

The fight was brief, broken up by friends or teachers, or it just fizzled out, my anger giving way to self-awareness and shame. I got violent because violence was a new, terrible economy: a quicker, surer way to give back the hurt. But by the end of it, I was so overcome with anger and regret that I was weeping, sobbing in deep heaves, struggling to breathe. I was suspended from school that day and the next.

My mother left work to pick me up. Through tears, I offered

her what seemed the natural defense: "He was talking about *you*." *Talking about*—another euphemism. My sense of dogged, retributive justice was all I could offer. If *it's just a joke* could, for young boys, calm heartache, *he was talking about you* could justify it. It felt strange to have lost, and to have lost my temper. Typically I was much cooler, more measured, I thought, but my hurt now was inconsolable. I haven't felt like that in a long time, perhaps since childhood, perhaps since that day.

In the car, my mother told me, "You don't have to defend me." I told her I knew that. Of course I did. But that bit of knowledge hadn't helped the sick feeling, the anger. "Did fighting help?" she asked. It hadn't, of course.

I didn't tell her what John said, what it was that had gotten to me. Here, I'll turn it around, see if I can get a rise now out of myself: my mother's so poor she can't even pay attention.

II

When I say I am a kissy drunk, we are on our second pitcher of flat Pabst, and we have swiveled on our barstools toward one another, our knees interlocking like a knuckle pound. I place that notion there between us, give it air. Wait to see whether it knocks over all this teetering prelude: we could go anywhere, do everything. The mood, the pitcher: these provide us that naive leeway, that hint of purpose to our evening. But we go nowhere, at least not together. Instead we stay a little longer at the bar before each exiting in different directions. In that time we gradually come to kissing shyly in our seats, attempting discretion, but, in that wide public spot, not having it at all.

/

Today's deflation: is it the hangover or something, anything, else? Last night my great friend and I met for drinks. You have a few and then a few more. So it goes. Then you step out for a cigarette, the chill and smoke, the whole thing of the city-night: other folks walking by, walking their dogs, walking from one place to anywhere else, and you in the middle of it, still, like a caesura.

/

She speaks of me as though I'm not there, or simply not paying attention. Refers to me as "this one," typically while playfully deriding me somehow. She cuts her eyes in my direction just as her tongue tip touches the roof of her mouth, humming out the nasal *N*. This is how I know she is flirting with me, even though I do not know if she is flirting with me. Either way I feel flirted with, tried for. Goaded. And regardless of what is or isn't the case, when she says it like that—"this one"—I want to be there, in the middle of that *N* sound, on her tongue, whole for a moment, like a lozenge, then dissolved, devoured. Whatever could happen (or will, or won't) is irrelevant, wrapped up as I am—and lost now—in the thought of that.

/

I feel occasionally outside myself with longing.

A strange thing to think, to feel.

Desire tends otherwise to be so bodily: I am a body, and you.

But here I am without all that.

/

I see myself obscured into someone I cannot stand to be: unbecoming, oafish, base. And not only in the distant past: my childhood for instance, a mullet cut into my hair, my Southern accent thick; nor in teenage stretches of booming ego and brashness that seem so foreign now; but even a month ago, a week, a day—I seem always a step behind my own criticisms, arguing with myself about my actions, even only a second after the fact.

/

Memory is a backward region.

/

Regret, as an emotional texture: it affects me differently than guilt or sadness does, or any other similarly lacerating mood. It's not that replaying the slow and hurtful end of a past love leaves me feeling as though I've done something wrong. I *know* I could have done something differently. Occasional mis-rememberings aside, the idea that *I could have* persists.

/

I could have stayed the night, instead of slipping out behind the ink cloud of an early morning obligation. I could have taken that job instead of backing out. I could have taken that trip. I could have apologized. I could have done a lot of things, but didn't, or I could have done what I did do, but differently. What could have been: my father could have stuck around. Or I could have taken him up on his offer, which he made a few years back, to get a beer sometime. I still could.

"Lord knows what my family has told you," he wrote, then. He stressed the importance of meeting—as men—to talk. Did I write back? What could I have said?

Just now, outside my window: a child's cry, a parent's scolding voice.

/

Regret: a skin on my skin.

/

Tonight I have one drink, another, another—what's the harm? My grandfather, soon after my grandmother's death, would close down his regular spot, Old Timers. They served chilidogs with chopped onions and slaw, cold beer. I'd wake in the middle of the night, call his car phone from the landline, its phone number scratched on an index card.

A strange voice would answer.

"Dad?" I'd say. I called him that in part to mirror the young aunts and uncles I grew up alongside, but also, I think, to fill in that gnawing gap in my diction.

"Bill? No, Bill can't talk now."

I'd hear his voice.

I'd hang up, go back to bed, and in the morning a paper bag of drive through food would await me on the kitchen counter.

You think, at first: this is what grief looks like.

Then, later: no, this is avoidance.

I close my tab: "What's the damage?"

/

In the past moment or so, the sundown has erased the city outside the train's window, rendered it flat black, a cool platitude.

I can barely see my reflection in the glass, and every now and again the yellow orbs of streetlights stitched along the city's stretching, diagonal avenues frame my face like a Hollywood vanity.

/

On the train, a man's face is identical to mine, just older. A touch more weary, or virile, or both. Does he see this in me? Does he see me at all?

The conflict: he has known his youthful face—he has known it in photographs, in mirrors—he knows it whether it, here, in me, insists or not. He could look at me and say yes or no. But I look at him and have to wonder at myself.

Actually, looking again, no: I see the tired, distant face of my father. A phantom face, a face I haven't seen at all, like a phantom limb: my brain pinpointing all that misplaced itch.

/

Down the block, I have a small coffee, some cream—

All these gorgeous dark-haired girls and the sun in my eyes.

/

I see a woman, her pale legs new in the early spring.

Rilke slips aptly into the middle of the day.

The look puts me elsewhere.

My eyes are on her, but my mind is deep in the wide volume of collected poems on the red, lacquered shelf by my writing desk:

Are there no places on your dear body
that keep remembering like eyes.

/

I stammer often, sometimes doubling back five words or more before beginning it all again, as though some impossible nag in my language has caught the tongue mid-sentence, has compelled me to reassess and begin again.

Barthes: *Language is a skin: I rub my language against the other.*

/

How to soften a poet.

/

Now I want to winnow down my exact feeling, give it a better name than *sideswiped*. Sadness, in a single, small dose.

Though, it's dense, layered like a punch line: regretting regret.

/

The Panopticon of a city street: always someone *implicitly* watching, always the possibility of being seen.

/

A man in the coffee shop sits with one hand on his chin, tugging the skin lightly, pinching his face as though dreaming. He wears his idleness, his unease at unoccupied hands, as a patch of red along his jaw, skin agitated by touching, rubbing, fending off the incredible stillness of a look. The intensity of his own gaze marks him, and the irony that it may fade before he has a chance to spy his own reflection is madding. As is the fact that, watching him so intently from my seat across the room, I've lost myself in a dream of what his day might further be—he'll soon stand, gather his pad of yellow paper and small book into the leather satchel by his feet, and go wherever one does in the early afternoon, when everyone and everything else seems so preoccupied—and in doing so have begun to touch my face as well.

The feel of my own stubble—my face in my hand. I hope to enjoy this incessantly, therefore apply the possessive frantically as though to prevent it ever flitting away: *my, my, my.*

/

A bad habit: I look into the glass of each storefront whenever I'm out on a walk, looking briefly at myself in each window's semi-reflection. It might seem like I'm drawn inside, like I'm surveying whatever goods sit there on display, but more often it's to check my posture, my stride, gauge a quick profile of my hair. Out walking with AB, or with one of my friends—anyone, really—I joke about this, which is to say simply mention it: it's funny enough an idiosyncrasy without having to lay into it with too much spin.

/

I guess I want to know: how do I look?

With my eyes, and in another's.

The gaze is recursive, like two mirrors bouncing their nested images back and forth ad infinitum, nauseam.

Eyes go: in the direction of a lover, a stranger, an object, a memory—

but finally, always, my gaze arrives at me.

/

Desire, worn like a dress.

/

Memory. This is how it goes: it goes.

/

I remember the story of my great-grandmother's first confession. She and the other girls were made to write their sins on little paper slips to help ease the shame of revealing one's transgressions, no matter how minor, for the first time. And instead of speaking them aloud to the priest, they were herded one by one into a small booth hemmed in by thick curtains and each girl was instructed, at the priest's word, to slide her hand up beneath the fabric and show him her sin.

/

AB seems to have a deeper tap, sometimes, on her past than should be possible. She calls me into the bedroom to ask some inconsequential favor, and I can see that she's been crying just a bit. "What's wrong?" She hides her eyes. She always hides her eyes for shame of being seen affected so deeply by whatever-it-is-this-time, as she says. This trivialization is her own thing. She tells me to look away even though I feel closer to her now than I typically do. I try to tell her this, but not in these words, not nearly at all. "Don't hide your face. Let me see. It's OK. What is it?" These words feel limp, actually, and don't say a thing at all about closeness. She's been watching a movie, and in some scene a hat reminiscent of one her grandfather had given to her before he died appeared on the head of a supporting character. She was overcome immediately with guilt: the feeling that, throwing it out some years ago during a move, she'd done something terribly wrong. But also regret: fixation on the poor choice, the feeling that something could have gone differently, should have gone differently, but didn't, and now in hindsight can't. I say what's done is done, because that's what you say—even though it's not done. It only ever seems that way, until you're watching a movie and it floors you again. And the worst part is how it hangs around, settles in like a stomach bug. What can you do? Get distracted, or numb, wait for something else to come along to ease off the dyspeptic burn: a joke, something to do with your hands. My grandfather would've been 70 today, and I hadn't thought of this until just now. I don't feel any specific way, certainly not the anguish AB had been feeling a second ago, and this disappoints me. AB remarks about how young he'd still be. I don't know if he ever wore a hat. I remember she'd wanted some water. That's why she called me in. I go and get her some.

/

Late last night, I sat in our dark bed while AB lay snoozing. Looking through the window, opened slightly to draw in some of the breeze, I had a feeling I sometimes have, as though the narrative line of my life, the arc of moments strung together by memory, in memory, had snapped, and I was untethered from that easy teleology. I felt small. I felt squashed. Call it a panic attack. Call it a crisis. I was a young man in a room, feeling alone but not alone, staring out from the bricked canal of my building's breezeway, out across the street, and beyond that through the alley opposite. I wondered what I was doing with myself. I wondered what building the brick wall I could see through the alley belonged to. I wondered what anyone else was doing. A siren somewhere, a window slides up.

III

THE MALE GAZE

Of course I looked.

It was the middle of the day, a Saturday in early spring, at the Starbucks not far from my apartment. Even though there are two, three other local shops within a short radius, this is one of my usual spots. The professional smiles and corporate-policy customer service make me feel completely anonymous. In places like those, one gets the feeling that this corner could be any corner anywhere, and I find that, for some reason, noirishly appealing, a kind of mass-commercial mystique. I walked in and went to make the requisite wide loop around the clump of easy chairs and short tables crowding the middle of the floor.

A young woman sat off to the side by a little booth made of two tables pushed together and bridged by what looked like a large tackle box packed with pots of paint. She was painting faces for a spring promotion, and when I stepped past, I slowed, and we made eye contact.

"I can do you like a cat," she said.

Beat.

"Or like Bowie."

She could sit me down, put her face close to mine and apply cream paint to my cheek with a white, plastic knife, which she held in her hand. She made a joke I can't remember about having forgotten her box of brushes, and I laughed and smiled and said something back that's lost to me now, something a bit suggestively coy, or coyly suggestive, and layered over with sarcasm, if I know myself at all.

I thought she was very pretty. She had olive skin and brown hair gathered up in a tight bun. Though, what was most alluring about her was the incredible *effortlessness* she exuded, as though staying there a while longer to speak with her more—about anything—was the only thing that mattered. She looked at me as though we'd known one another for some time, a hint of recognition around the edges of her smile. And she spoke to me easily, confidently, like we'd done this before and were simply picking up our conversation from where it last left off.

I typically have trouble telling flirtation from general friendliness, and for that reason I felt suddenly, sharply unsafe around her. My body showed it, probably: I made my joke and strode away backward, backpedaling, making a broad, bodily gesture like an overblown shrug or a theatrical bat of the hand—as though to say *Oh, stop. Keep going.*

At the counter, I put in my order sheepishly, though probably still sporting a little smile. As I milled back by her toward a bank of open seats, I watched her stand, bend forward, and reach down to rifle through a black canvas bag rumpled on the honey-colored travertine. Then, something torn clean from one of my adolescent fantasies happened: her leggings slid down, way down, and I got a good look.

The material, a glossy black, fell in thick folds beneath her short dress, also black, which she wore cinched around the waist with a thin patent leather belt. I slowed, and from where I stood, I could see her simple striped panties, cut like boy's shorts, and the backs of her pale thighs stark against all the monochrome. I remember this image more than I remember her face or the specifics of our little exchange.

She must've felt a draft, or maybe she felt the fabric's shifting tensions around her legs, because after a moment she gathered the leggings tightly in her fist, slid them up over her body and beneath her dress. She said something overly explanatory and overly loud as she did—"My leg just *itches*"—a way to deflect or conceal her embarrassment, or excuse all her obvious tugging at her underneaths. Though I can't know whether she was embarrassed. She didn't see me looking, I don't think, nor anyone else—if anyone else was. I just know that, had it been me with my clothes falling off, I would've felt embarrassed. Even as an onlooker, I felt embarrassed. I watched her wriggle from side to side with a quick, desperate utility that fully deflated my suffocating little bubble of desire.

The look itself felt more like a peek. I tilted my head to the side out of surprise and interest. I looked, looked away, then tried for a second glance. It lasted about a second. Probably less. The feeling of that moment's desire persists—a heavy, grasping hope that the fabric might slip a little more—but also, now, after the fact, I find myself forming a new desire particular to the business of memory: I want to see that moment again just as it was—and I can—but I also want to see it a little differently. I can replay it in my mind, picturing her bare skin again and again, imagining more or less of it if I want, shifting the details to suit my liking—and I do.

Many men, I think, presume to have perfected their methods for slipping a glance here or there when someone pretty walks by, but rarely is it as candid as one hopes. I sometimes watch the way other men react to attractive women.

You hear about "undressing with the eyes," but that's rarely what works for me. I tend to look *at* the clothes, not through. To note how their thicknesses conceal, or how they do not. How material hits the body beneath it, and that material's penchant to hug and stretch, or drape and play. What I like is how the clothes fall—and not *off*, but *around* a form. How the body is physical beneath leather, cotton, and wool, and how it secures those materials against sloughing themselves off, which I am always sure they are eager to do. The body also resists the ways cloth can hold, though, how its movements undress itself. And there I am, walking by and looking.

Typically I'm all for indulging the eye: I take a seat close to the window for precisely that reason, and spend long moments lost in thought watching cars and people go by. The street stays busy, stays moving, and thankfully so. But about that peek: my eyes felt so impossibly physical on her, as though through them, I pawed at the skin I'd focused on.

I looked, looked away, and then turned back for a second pass: surprise, shame, and then what felt like transgression. The second of second-guessing was a brief shot of panic at the realization that what had begun as play—the jokes, the smiles, the could-be flirting—had turned somehow more serious. When wanting gets so quickly, maybe even neatly, satisfied, when desire is so easily fulfilled, fantasy gets pulled through reality like stuffing from a pillow's busted seam. There's an inversion of inside and outside—that safe, soft dichotomy ruptures—and it baffles you a little bit. And though the feeling I anticipated in that moment was glee, the actual response was panic, and I suffered a sort of contrapasso: I felt punished by what I'd wanted.

Of course I looked: because I'm allowed to—expected to, even—and because, not only did I want to look, I'm not sure how not to. It really is such a thrill, that first little glance. It's something I learned—and learned to appreciate—early, as soon as I learned that boys and girls were different: that boys looked, and girls got looked at. It took longer to learn, though, the burden that look lays on women and girls, the power it has, and the power it confirms. And, to go with that power: shame, with which I doubt I'll ever reconcile.

DO

"If you hurt me like that again," she said, "I'll stop speaking to you."

We were sitting with our legs tucked under us on her small blockish couch, watching *The Radiant Child* and kissing every so often. I was new in my beard, in that difficult middle stage between stubble and fullness where every stint, however long, before a mirror seems like a debate with one's reflection: *Shave it. No.* Fight or flight bearing down hard on commitment.

She said it coolly: "If you hurt me like that again . . . "

The phrase lay there a moment, like a gun in the first act. Of course I would hurt her again. We'd met one night at a bar, where we'd joked and laughed and touched just enough to feel together, in the moment, despite our strangeness toward one another and the incredible noise of the crowded room around us. At one point, the pivotal point, she kissed me suddenly, forcefully. I kissed back, and we continued kissing, brazenly, publicly, catching some sidelong glares, playing the part of *that* couple: too caught up in ourselves to be discreet.

As the weeks went on, it became clear that we were, in fact, that couple: all new and performative, displaying passion publicly to compensate for the null we experienced in private. We spent a short while seeing one another occasionally, spending time at my place or hers, maybe sitting down for coffee sometime, sharing some small plates at an early dinner, late lunch, however you like. Then I stopped calling her—I'm not sure why—and she called me, anyway. I spent a few months seeing other women, thinking not really at all about it other than entertaining every so often the idea that it was so blandly *typical* of me, such a stock, mannish thing to do, a fact that, though I resented it quite a bit, I had resigned myself to.

How was I so sure she'd see me as a heartbreaker like that? Was I just seeing myself that way? What could I do? Or, what would I? After a while, I called her again—why not?—and suggested that we see one another sometime, which we did again for a few weeks in ways strikingly similar to how we'd shared our time before: sneaking through her art school campus and into a music festival downtown, lying in bed for hours with the records on repeat, sharing a cupcake and playing Scrabble at a little cafe. We played well together, though something just wasn't there for me, and it was only a short time before I felt it again: the desire to do something different, see someone else, and so I did. Simple as that. I met another woman, at another bar, and began a habit of repeating myself, repeating my actions, repeating disappointment in myself.

If you hurt me like that again. It was a taunt, offered bluntly between kisses, a touch of play lining its sincerity. It felt inevitable that it should play out how it did, and the result was, in a way, irresistible because of that. This gave me a way to explain it, to say that I was behaving simply as men do: flightily, noncommittally. Though I never did explain—I just did it, slipped into the role. It was easier than having a conversation openly, there on her couch, about what I did and didn't like about her, or what she maybe did or didn't like about me. A conversation about why, in spurts, she seemed truly invested in me, and why I avoided her because of it.

Now that I think of it, she didn't say "hurt" at all, did she? She said "*do*." If you *do* that again. Her hurt was my assumption, though in fact she didn't seem hurt at all at the time. She seemed sure of herself, confident in her ultimatum. She kissed me, tasting a little like beer, putting her lips on one corner of my mouth, and then the other, back and forth a few times. I guess it's easier to assume she was hurt, and to apply all the blame that goes along with it. It helps make more sense, at least narratively, of the baffling fact that, from time to time, people just want to be with someone for a little while, and then they don't anymore.

That drunken tug toward a mouth pursed like an asterisk: who never felt it?

DRESS FORM

Here, overlooking my desk, stands a padded white torso. It is the approximation of a woman's body: a rigid dress form. This is in the little office space AB and I share across the narrow hall from our bedroom. I've got a bookshelf here, a wide, red, lacquered one. I keep paper slips, pens and pencils scattered throughout it and on my moddish white desk. She has her sewing notions, bolts of fabric, a pin cushion fashioned as a hard, green tomato, a tuft of darker green felt at the top like little leaves. And there's the dress form, backed into its corner like a mannequin, though soft-bodied, and without head and legs and arms, as though it's upped the Venus de Milo's ante. Mary McCarthy slept in the shadow of one of these as a child, and remarked that, almost always, it stood at least partially covered by a wrap or semblance of shawl for decorum's sake.

AB works her designs on it, stretching and draping fabric over and around its shoulders, its waist, dressing and undressing it with occasional tenderness, though more frequently with curt utility. Garments accrete slowly there, with very little ceremony, though often with heaping grievance. She'll spend a few hours carefully pinning a project to it, then, suffering some turn of thought or lapse in satisfaction, she'll take it all down, throw the fabric to the side in a ruffled clump. I watch her work sometimes. I'll stop in the doorway and lean against the jamb for a minute or more. Sometimes she smooths the fabric flat, brushing it down, perhaps picking away—almost lovingly—a bit of lint. Other times she yanks, grips, seems to strangle it in frustration.

All told, it's an easy form, a placeholder over which to slip a dress, a stock body to swaddle in organza and gauze, wool and looping bands of horsehair crinoline. It has a fuller figure than most, I'm told, because it is older—from some recently bygone period a handful of decades ago, during which time the expectations layered onto a woman's shape differed. It has wider hips, a bigger bust, is a little taller, too, I think. These stock forms are smaller now, less hip and less breast—less overall—to couch, I think, the last great desire of the fashion designer: that the model should disappear entirely, and the clothes somehow wear themselves.

There was a time, early puberty, when I would have been too timid to look at the dress form at all—the suggestion of breasts, the curve of buttocks: these would have been a little too much for me. Passing all the little boutiques down Central Avenue in Charlotte, on my walk home from the bus each day, I would turn my eyes away from the sight of clerks swapping outfits on mannequins in window displays. Partly because of the brazenness of their bare, enameled bodies—and this was during a time when most featured small, sculpted nipples—partly because I felt a little *too* drawn to look, but some imprinted Southern sensibility spoke up, urged me toward primness. I'd sneak a glance, sure—just one; good measure—then shuffle past, my eyes on the tips of my tennis shoes.

Something about this seems like such a fitting metaphor for a first glimpse at longing in my life: the object, a woman's form beyond a pane of glass, flattened like a platitude, and of course entirely constructed, faked, yet thrilling nevertheless. I found that same thrill collecting and looking at magazine clippings of actresses in scooped, form-fitting ball gowns, or swimsuit models all tanned and airbrushed, which I kept hidden by my bed in one of my mother's discarded guest checkbooks from her serving job.

Like most straight little boys, learning how to perform my sexuality meant first learning how to look.

To feel a little closer to AB, I began learning to sew not very long ago, setting myself down at a sewing machine—in this same spot here in the office, in fact—for a hasty once-over. AB showed me. I learned what I learned quickly enough, despite some mild unease. I tend to rush instructions, trying to gather too quickly the choreography of complicated tasks. I made sure to cover it with a protective, bluffing scrim: *Yeah, sure, sure, I got it, yeah, OK*—while, inside, I was panicking just a bit, struggling to commit each step to a more meaningful kind of memory, to learn the mechanical contours of this slick white thing, its fickle little tendencies.

But before that, I picked up a good portion of what I know in scraps and tidbits breadcrumbed through any given day, just listening to AB talk about her work. Learning a new vocabulary is, and maybe has always been, a thing of great amusement for me: very often the words aren't *new*, really, just the same old bit more brilliant because of it. *Tension* and *allowance* mean more with cloth in hand than they did before. Much of the seamster's lexicon feels whimsical—*bobbin, spool, zipper foot* and the like—though it's also run-through with implications of violence, which shears clean off from all that sharp action: needles, pins, scissors, and rippers.

French seam is one phrase that seemed plain at first. AB was telling me about a piece she'd been working on, a sort of asymmetrical tank made of tealish organza. *Something something French seam.* I asked her what it meant, what it looked like, because I couldn't picture it for myself. I watched closely her sure, quick hands pantomiming the needle's push and jerk, explaining: lay the fabric's plain sides, the wrong sides, together. Stitch down the edge. Open the sewn panel, trim the seam neat and press it open with an iron. Then fold the whole business back the other way, right sides together, and stitch it again, hiding the raw edge inside.

It's just a way of hiding the seam, a tactic best applied to sheer things. As is often the case, you do more work to try to hide the fact that you've done anything at all. But my imagination tore it open, and the words became like a pocket turned out. And I was just stunned for a moment, hooked by the hard truth that there are some things I shouldn't keep to myself.

On the dress form now is a wool number the steely color of cold things, a thoughtful gray-blue, with a band of lighter crinoline that loops around the neck and dances down the back seam. This particular dress lives in-and-out of a garment bag latched to the back of the closet door, and only occasionally adorns the dress form. When it's out, when AB slips it over the dress form to make little alterations or simply to look at it, I look too. And, actually, I touch. The curatorial quality of a thing on display like that litters the moment of contact—fingers on fabric—with taboo. The wool is dense, felt-like. The crinoline is a springy mesh that turns and bows like a Möbius strip. Touching it, I feel as though I'm touching another woman, and the figure of the dress form filling it out doesn't help much to slow that steady-swelling association. To touch anything that way, though, to touch in order to feel, to *really* feel, is such an extension of the self, of a desire to test the

71

outer bounds of oneself—skin on *something*—that it is difficult to deny at least a tinge of intimacy. It's so delicate, that touch: a way of using my hands reserved typically for the small of a back or the hair swung loosely over an ear. Her ear.

How would it seem if, in one of these moments, someone happened upon me touching the dress? If, walking past, they paused at the door the way I do sometimes? I'd shrink away, I think. I'd attempt to put on a sort of expertise, or at least semi-professional curiosity, to clumsily shield myself from the onlooker's gaze. There in the office, running my hands delicately over this dress worn by a phantom woman's form, touching it just to touch: I worry it would seem seedy, unbecoming. My sense of shame, never fully shed since childhood, would well up, and I'd step back, shoot my eyes toward my shoes.

But that's not all, actually. I'm realizing it now: on some level I touch it to feel closer to her craft—which she cares so deeply about and works so steadily toward—and through that, closer to her. And the most pressing concern is that, once caught, instead of smiling and saying firmly, proudly, *AB made this*, and letting that good fact be reason enough to warrant my curiosity, my love to touch, I'd flounder instead. Feel ashamed. Of what, exactly? Such honest, open affection, which for whatever reason I've always kept tucked away and guarded for fear of being splayed open. And what's worse is that I worry that it would be AB to stumble upon me, alone in our office, touching her dress, and that instead of looking her straight in the face and saying what I want, *I love you*, I'd displace that desire, try to shy away from it, distance myself from it, or hide it altogether.

THE ALLURE OF THE CUT

I like the chef's knife, its broad blade like a smile. AB prefers one of the many slim, serrated knives with wooden handles that crowd the drawer, six or seven of them huddled there. She cuts in her hand, not on the board as I do. She slides the blade through the slick flesh of a tomato or cucumber, pulling the knife toward her thumb. I try for technique: slowly, awkwardly even, measuring cuts with the tip of the knife in quick tugging motions, or pushing the heel down and away for a proper chop. She'll crowd a small plate with the fat, wet chunks, or thumb them directly into a wide wooden salad bowl. I categorize and arrange the cut parts in little piles across the cutting board. What does this say about me? I tend to be concentrated, stubborn, technical in most things. I take pleasure in procedure, get squeamish in its absence. What does it say about her? She trusts in her abilities more than in any knowledge of a right or wrong way—never a quick slip into the knuckle to sheer off a thin wing of opaque skin, never a name for technique beyond *How my grandmother did it*.

I love that she and I differ on this. We have built what we have on food—partnership, a home, a way to love and hate in moments: preparing it ourselves, all atop one another's toes in the kitchen; sifting through a long menu, deciding, then smiling across a table until it comes and we can nitpick how a dish stacks up—discussing acid and fat, what cuts and what gets cut; prying open a brown delivery bag, messy, cross-legged on the floor, to find fried wantons and tofu soaked in sweet, spicy peanut sauce, little steaming cups of rice, and packets of soy to hoard indefinitely in a wooden bowl in the pantry.

She says it's an old world way, cutting in her hands, which could mean either the hills of Italy or of West Virginia. I use words like *julienne* and *brunoise* because they signify to me a kind of trained excellence that I long for. I'm all militant *mise-en-place* to her on-the-fly, heaping, rustic arrays. Because of this, I'm often so particular, so know-it-all, that I have to look away when she takes into her sure hand an onion, roughly carves out a wedge of its bawdy, white layers. My fear that she'll cut herself just because I watch is too irrational. My urge to comment on what she does, and how, is too great. I lower my eyes. I leave the room.

I have a tattoo of a semicolon above the inside of my right elbow. As I lay under the hot lights of the tattoo parlor, I had expected the needle's touch to feel more surgical. Even though I knew the stuttering tattoo gun's movement on my skin comprised thousands of minuscule pricks, I could not help but relate that sort of staid deliberation—the tattooist's leveled focus; the firm, gloved hands; the antiseptic tinge of rubbing alcohol; the controlled breaking of skin—to going under the knife. I think that was my way of adding some importance to the moment, which in reality was the result of impulse. It was the first warm Friday of spring, and there was nothing to do. My friends and I were all in an odd place of upheaval. I was a month or so clear of an extended, complicated breakup with a girl I'd moved in with far too quickly. Two other friends were entering into a series of fights and disappointments that would result in the end of their own relationship. And another friend's marriage had just collapsed. Mostly we were all bored.

Sometimes when I write the word *marriage*, I read it instead as *marrage*, which is not actually a word. Though, if it were, it would be some noun form of "mar": the remnants of damage done, or maybe the act of damaging itself. Nobody says "my marriage" until that marriage has ended.

Around age ten, some time after my mother's second divorce, and after she'd tried out relationships with a few equally unfulfilling guys, I punched through a pane of glass in my bedroom window—just to see if I could, or to see what would happen. I shadow boxed three quick jabs at the window before cocking back, pivoting around my waist a bit, and putting my little fist through the glass. It broke clean through, most of it, though a small shard caught the inside of my wrist and scooped out a flap of skin about the size of a nickel. I stood dumbly for what seemed like too long, just looking. I could see pale tissue there, inside. For a while there wasn't much blood, just a throbbing unlike the familiar sting that goes along with minor nicks and paper cuts. The scar it left looks like a navel—a tightly wound knot of skin. I was acting out. It took me some years to realize this, to shed my earlier explanation that I'd simply been home alone and bored. It was some time before the window was fixed—the better part of a year, I think.

I want to call it sensual, the way AB stands at the cutting board: her hands clasped close to her chest, fingers delicately guiding the blade through the slick flesh of a tomato or cucumber. The way the knife's saw-edge presses lightly into the meat of her thumb, the way its little teeth just barely depress the skin, the way the severed fruit lops off into the bowl. It's unbearable how lovely and fraught that touch can seem from across a dusky kitchen. I want to be with her because I love her, and I feel that I will forever. Though, isn't that the nature of love? Love, when you've got it, feels permanent: the beginning long forgotten or muddled, the end inconceivable. Sometimes I want to say *I want to get married*. But that phrase, a declaration disguising a request, is hushed by my dread of embarrassment. Of what? Of love. I learned somehow that eagerness to share affections beyond the physical was a quality to avoid, that to too quickly, too willfully expose my emotions was to open myself up to destruction. She could say *I don't*, and that would be that. I push here and there at what I'm willing to hope for, imagining a moment years from now, a moment quite like this—she, not very far from me, sewing or reading or just sitting—a moment colored by a particular feeling: *we wanted this so many years ago, pictured it even, and now we've got it*. What is it I want? The passage of time. But I'm still at the door to the kitchen. And she hasn't looked up.

I have always had a kind of proletarian reverence for knives—
do all little boys? One evening while my mother worked late, or
maybe had a date, a pair of her friends had me over to watch me
for the night. The woman was a server like my mother. The man
was a chef at some other restaurant. He and I cooked together
that night in preparation for a school fair to which each student
was charged to bring a homemade dessert. I always squirmed
at the thought of craft fairs or special event days at school, and
honed my neurosis in the days leading up to them. They seemed
unfair expositions of home life thrust into the sickly-lit showroom
of a small gymnasium. Anything that required parental assistance
or the input of extra cash into some school day extravagance
designed to lift spirits and enrich the lives of students had the
opposite effect: I fixated on the money needed, refused to ask,
didn't dare mention—for no reason other than my own worry at
seeming needy—that I needed my mother to spend her evening
not at work, but at home, painting something with me, helping
me cook her mother's Brown Betty to feed to the girls and boys
at school. That night, as my mother's friend and I sliced apples at
the counter, he told me that a knife's blade should be revered, like
God himself: never drop it, never abuse it, always keep it sharp.
Even then, I gathered that his rhetoric seemed a touch extreme,
though this did nothing to calm my excitement at so severe, so
flippant, a comparison. Suddenly the small paring knife in my
hand, the substantially larger chef's knife in his: these seemed
impossibly important.

Cutting cabbage for slaw some time ago, I nicked my finger, flayed a good chunk of the middle knuckle clean away from the bone. AB was washing the dishes quietly behind me when it happened, and I left the kitchen with no explanation. There was no romanticizing the blade then, just sternly setting the knife aside, probably a severe look on my face, and plodding into the bathroom to dig for Band-Aids. Just her calling from the kitchen to ask whether, if I dipped into the bedroom, I could bring her my coffee cup from our bedside table. And just me barking back, wanting at that moment nothing to do with her at all, and for no real reason beyond the panic of hurt flesh: "No. No. Just leave me alone for a second, OK? OK?"

ECONOMY

Though it's been a few years, my mind is hung up now on a check I wrote one fall, a check to repay a personal debt to a friend, $150 or so—a friend I lost, and a check that bounced.

I'd been in a bad way money-wise over the summer, and borrowed the little bit of money from her to help ease the strain of my bills. She and I had been fiercely close, and she agreed to help me immediately, discreetly, sensitive to my discomfort over having had to ask. She let the debt float a little while—for a few months, during which time our closeness became fiercer and fiercer, and, actually, we began sleeping together. We developed a habit of slipping away semi-secretly from our friends one or two nights a week as we sat at a bar or capping the night over beers in someone's den. We'd head out separately, pretending to yawn and rub our eyes, yet with plans to meet up in an hour or so at another spot. After a while, though, I started slipping away from her, too. She and I never put a name to what we were doing—a fact I held as tightly to my chest as possible. There were other girls for a while, each with their own ups and downs, but after a while I came to realize—or recognize, rather—that she had begun to love me. Or perhaps already did. By this point, though, I was too far gone, too unnerved by the thought of making real what I had erringly thought of as *play*. It terrified me—and I stayed away.

I wrote her the check, I signed it, dated it, and tore it from its little faux-leather book, and I slid it into her hand. If she had anything to say to me, I've forgotten what it was. We stood in the hallway of a big building downtown, where I'd gone to meet her at work. It was a cold, quick exchange. After, I left the city. I tagged along on a trip north into Wisconsin to camp with a few of our common friends for the weekend. They had wanted to see to some sort of outing before the weather turned too cool to warrant it, and I was desperate for a change of place.

The day of the trip, a sense of otherness clung to me in the car, instigated partly by my money worries, partly by the looming question of whether I should've stayed behind and tended to the damage I'd done. My friends, bickering over the radio station, chatting about their weeks: their moods seemed untouchable to me, even though I was only inches away. I kept my eyes out the window, where the fields and farmlands flitting by distracted me, at least at first. But I was feeling down, remorseful, and a mood like that isn't so easily shaken.

I cracked my window to let in a little of the cool September, hoping to draw up some of the rough smells of livestock, dirt patches, dry leaves. These always remind me of car trips through rural Carolina to pick up or drop off my brother at his father's house—how I'd hang my hand out the window, into the air and sun, or the cool dark, depending, and listen to the crickets stirring, to the sound of the car as it tore away through all the air around it. They signal freshness to me, typically, but as I sat in my fitted denim, my boots, and my flannel, I felt a sharp pang of remorse. What was I doing there? Poor decisions had seemed to compound upon one another at that moment in my life, and all the while I had nothing really to show for it. I felt gutted by the feeling that I, now a man moving into the clumsiness of quarter-life, had nothing to say for myself, for my behaviors, and certainly had much less to show. "We're through," she'd said. "You owe me money."

The children of the working poor are, from a young age and on, groomed for wistfulness, dutiful stoicism, and resignation to that fact that it falls on them to carry the hardness of their family's myth—remembering their mothers' and fathers' tired forms with their own small muscles, feeling a grandfather's ache in their own little bones. In my family, the rough edge of poverty got gradually encased by folksy charm and misremembered quaintness. Third- and fourth-run hand-me-downs and elastic, megastore short sets were, as we got older, something for us to remember fondly as builders of character. Descriptions of my grandmother's thrifty dinners designed to feed seven or eight—packaged noodles and buttered white bread, or seventy-nine-cent tins of Vienna sausages—became conversation fodder to recall fondly at holidays or family get-togethers. My mother called the unemployment checks she collected for the better part of a year—$300 a week—a pittance, yet in good humor, joking all the while about her champagne tastes.

Later that night, we made our camp in one of those common, convenient state-maintained recreational areas—this one boasting its status as "largest maintained prairie in the state" on an etched wooden sign. We set a boxy, nylon tent for the four of us at the top of a short, gravel drive. At the nearby supermarket, my friends loaded a shopping cart full: slabbish boxes of beer, cheap pats of ground beef in white Styrofoam trays, dense wheat crackers, and jars of cadmium-colored pub cheese—and I just sort of lagged silently behind the whole procession, hoping to turn invisible, to avoid a conversation about not being able to chip in, and why.

We gathered firewood from a free, tarp-covered stack at the side of a nearby farmhouse, and burned it through the night, staying up late and drinking cold cans of beer. I found myself a little giddy at the fact of just being here, which was a welcome, if slight, relief from the morose, nervous texture of the previous day. Before long, I got to doing math on my fingers as we sat around the fire. The check was going to bounce: I knew this, yet felt driven to reaffirm it. I counted again, noting every little expense, every eager deposit. It was paper bluff. When the fire settled down to its fiercely hot coals—orange cubes white with ash, like a dense packet of Turkish delight—we took turns idly flicking pocket change into the embers, prodding a hot nickel or dime with the pointed tip of a stick. At some high temperature, a good press to the center of a coin will crumple the president's face into a small, marred hunk, like a pop top, and flame up bright blue. Beyond the impracticality of that act, the wastefulness, it's the irreverence that still sits guiltily with me: to burn money. Why on earth? If there's a single thing I've come to fetishize above all other things in my life, it's what has always seemed exotic, fleeting, powerful and fragile like a lover's body: it is the dollar bill.

Some moments—some memories of moments—seem unshakable in their persistence, and find ways to thread themselves again and again through the better part of an hour, a day, a weekend. I spent the next afternoon on a graying, wooden picnic bench a few steps into the grass from the zippered front of our tent, trying to remember Thoreau a little bit, trying to feel a little more exterior, less burdened by myself. I used to joke that "Economy" is *Walden*'s longest section, thumbing my nose a bit at the irony. I revisit one passage sometimes, reading it aloud to feel each clause build and build upon the others:

> It is very evident what mean and sneaking lives many of you live, for my sight has been whetted by experience; always on the limits, trying to get into business and trying to get out of debt [. . .] still living, and dying, and buried by this other's brass; always promising to pay, promising to pay, tomorrow, and dying today, insolvent [. . .] making yourselves sick, that you may lay up something against a sick day, something to be tucked away in an old chest, or in a stocking behind the plastering, or, more safely, in the brick bank; no matter where, no matter how much or how little.

That bit about "what mean and sneaking lives" the poor must live, I resented it on my first reading, failing to see that, despite its paternalistic airs, it has a sympathetic bent. I've been told I spend money "like a poor person": immediately, impulsively, until it's gone. I'd like not to believe I do, though my habits seem to speak otherwise. I hate the feeling it draws up: helplessness, as the potential for poverty sits in me like a predisposition toward cancer. When I was nine or ten, I used to hang on my mother's sleeve at the store, pointing out bright packages of candy or boxes of cereal, saying, "When we have money, Mom, can we get this? When we have money?" How that must have crushed her: that I knew not to *directly* ask for what I saw—the answer would've been "No"—but that I still couldn't help my wanting.

I wish I could've known this then: that check was a Dear Jane letter, of sorts. I had, by then, met AB, and we had begun a period of heavy flirting—playful cattiness, half-hearted attempts at getting coffee, a beer, what have you—which would result not only in the full-on breaking of my friend's heart, but the beginning of the most serious and long-term relationship I've ever had. When, after two nights, the group of us broke camp and returned to the city, it seemed a decided fact that there was nothing left to say. The hurt was clear, though. And, so I came to see later, was one resounding question: why not me? The check did bounce, but there was never another word about it.

CODA

DESIRE

Years ago I was dating a girl named Julia, one of the great early and fleeting loves of my life, whose parents divorced in the months after we'd gotten together. It was hard on her, obviously, especially as it happened in her first semester away at school. I offered support, in what meager way I could, but found myself unable to do much more than nod along as she vented and cried. One of the only constants in my parents' relationship is that they've never, in my life, been together. What could I say to comfort her?

One spring, we visited her father's lake cabin in the uplands of west Georgia, a mountainous part of the state I'd never known existed prior to going there, envisioning only lowlands of red clay and post-plantation farm country instead. Her father and his new girlfriend suggested Julia and I try the newly installed steam shower, a little luxury symptom of his grapples with midlife. "It's wonderful to have someone scrub your back," they offered. "Use the sugar scrub." I knew immediately such intimate knowledge could only come through the experience of having done it themselves. Julia and I eyed one another warily. They didn't relent. What did I make of it? The whole thing had a baffling vibe. Maybe I was uncomfortable with their insistence, expecting a trap to be sprung as soon as I moved to the shower, her father testing my manners and intentions. Maybe I was put off by how cloying it seemed: her father struggling to offer some version of *the other side* in contrast to her mother's home, where we were forbidden from so much as sharing a bedroom. Maybe her father and his girlfriend just felt too familiar, trying to join in some idea of the youthful relationship, in which exuberance often undoes discretion.

In sixth grade, gobs of us would sit with our puppy loves on the steps after school, one couple daring another to kiss, and so on, and so on, and such taunting goaded us into our first experiences of another's body: awkward, hurried, and minding always the performance, which was perhaps more essential to the scene than any sincere desire to kiss. Of course we wanted to, we always wanted to—but in those moments we got to. Had to, really, weighed down by the dare. I once whispered a request into the ear of a friend: he should dare my then girlfriend and me to kiss, *really* kiss, for some number of seconds. He did. And I looked to her and shrugged—"Well, we have to . . ."—and leaned in. And she leaned back. And we both knew how constructed it was, I think, though that didn't lessen my capacity to have a good time, my mouth on hers, my tongue awkwardly mashing against her face.

With Julia, though, it was different. She and I stepped into the steam unceremoniously, unexcitedly. We felt we had to, so we touched one another's bodies, though we did so lightly, numbly, whatever pleasure we might have found diminished by having been told precisely where it lay, how to get it. Later in the night, her father and his girlfriend slipped into the outdoor tub together with a bottle of chardonnay. To what extent was it a *shared* awkwardness, this coarse untethered romance? Maybe they felt just as odd as us. Beneath this moment stirs something that still makes me shift uncomfortably: that I'd been made somehow accessory, that I had been given the *repayment*—if one could call the awkward shower that—ahead of the favor: as if he'd said *don't tell Julia's mother about us, and I won't say a thing either.*

I did use the sugar scrub—scooped it from its squat jar with two fingers, scraped it into my palm. I laugh a little now, thinking about that. It seemed like solid advice, and maybe I wasn't so totally resolved to resist her father's encouragement as I imagine myself to have been. *Well, we have to . . .* But as I applied it to her back, I found myself doing so listlessly, in a *told* way—the way, as a boy, I emptied the trash or did the dishes when commanded, dragging the strained black mass of plastic across the kitchen floor, throwing away forks too caked with food to warrant the hard work of scrubbing. Despite her father's overbearing approval, it still felt so *transgressive* to touch her: the private moment invaded by the guilt of—even there, concealed as we were, hidden— *insolence*. How can it be that in a moment of such demanded, such *insisted* adulthood—*go, be alone together, naked, wet, with our best wishes*—one feels most of all like a child?

DEBTS

This book would have been impossible, really, without the encouragement and crucial eye of Colleen O'Connor, who is one of my dearest friends and most talented peers. Special thanks also to my great teachers Jenny Boully and Aviya Kushner, who helped coax many of these essays into existence.

David Lazar's guidance and tough love have been invaluable in my development as an essayist. I cannot stress this enough. A thousand thanks to him for believing in what my work could be—ever since, regarding one piece that simply wasn't *getting there*, he said, "It has to *perform* something. It has to *say* something. Otherwise, it's just a fuckin' story."

Thank you to the editors at The Lettered Streets Press: Abigail Zimmer, Joshua Young, and especially Ian Denning, who worked ferociously to make this book what it is.

An early version of "Desire" appeared originally in *Ghost Proposal* No. 3.

There appear, in these essays, some quotations whose original authors or texts are acknowledged to varying degrees. In the name of full transparency, here they are compiled:

p. 12, this line from Mencken is just one of those widely-quoted quips that wind up peppering the collective unconscious, like a standard put down in a commonplace book. I'm not sure where it first appeared, nor where I first heard it.

p. 13, the Psalm mentioned here is Psalm 23. Verse 5, specifically. King James Version.

p. 19, *The Notebooks of Malte Laurids Brigge*, translated by Michael Hulse.

p. 26, this is from Beerbohm's wonderful essay "Dandies and Dandies."

p. 31, Barthes's bit on the "spectacle of excess" is from his essay "The World of Wrestling," in *Mythologies*, translated by Annette Lavers.

p. 51, the Rilke here is from an untitled poem, which appears in his *Uncollected Poems*, compiled and translated by Edward Snow.

p. 52, this Barthes is from *A Lover's Discourse: Fragments*, translated by Richard Howard.

p. 84, this is, of course, from "Economy" in Thoreau's *Walden*.

xo

BIO

Ryan Spooner is an Assistant Editor at Essay Press. His essays have appeared in *Ghost Proposal, South Loop Review,* and *CutBank,* whose Big Fish Lyric Essay contest he won in 2011. He lives in Chicago, where he teaches writing and literature.

COLOPHON

This book was designed and typeset in 10.5 point Baskerville, the titles in 18 point Baskerville and 16 point Arial fonts. The cover is printed on Mohawk Via Felt and the interior is printed on Accent Opaque stock. Printing sourced by The Lettered Streets Press.

OTHER TLSP BOOKS

Supper & Repair Kit by Nicole Wilson (2014)

Split Series Volume I [*This Will Be His Legacy* by Aubrey Hirsch
    & *Bone Matter* by Alexis Pope] (2014)

The Blank Target by Robert Alan Wendeborn (2015)

Split Series Volume II [*Birds As Leaves* by Melanie Sweeney
    & *Seven Sunsets* by Jasmine Dreame Wagner] (2015)